A Gift For

From

Rise and Be Healed

Poems Inspired by the Miracles
of
Jesus Christ, Our Lord

Barbara Caldwell Adkins

Rise and Be Healed
by Barbara Caldwell Adkins

Printed in the United States of America

ISBN 1-60034-531-X

www.xulonpress.com

Contents

I dedicate this book to my precious family,

Marvin, Scott, Ali, and Cathy.

With all my love

Preface

The vision of an angel at the pool of Bethesda troubling the water for healing was so vivid to me. It consumed my mind as I left the indoor pool, returned home, and reread John's account of Jesus' healing an invalid. I am amazed that for 38 years a man would seek healing and not lose hope. His faith strengthened my faith. Then my first miracle poem, "The Gospel Must be Heard", was born. The last verse inspired me to continue writing.

Believe and strongly witness!
Proclaim the sacred Word!
Refuse to sit in silence!
The Gospel must be heard!

I remembered the chart of miracles I had seen in my great-grandmother's Bible. With awe I opened the well-worn, yellowed pages to find the miracles listed in the order Jesus performed them. God had provided me with a guide to research the miracles. (These scripture references are found in the endnotes.) Also, taken from my great-grandmother's Bible, and found at the end of this book, is a summary of the miracles by category: Supply, Healing, Exorcising Devils,

Judgment, Deliverance, and Raising the Dead. There are more miracles of Healing than any other.

I was greatly inspired by the Lord to write this poetry. Before I put pen to paper, I read the Scriptures, prayed and meditated. Then the words I needed came easily, and as I was writing the Lord would often reply. Please note the words in italics are mine, all others, I know, were given to me by God. This book is a very personal account of our relationship. I could not have written this poetry without His hand in mine.

Dr. Charles L. Allen, beloved Methodist pastor and author, greatly encouraged me to compile these poems into a book. Dr. Allen died in the fall of 2005. My friend Bill Wagner gave me the title, *Rise and Be Healed.* My poem, "Rise and Be Healed", is a tribute to Bill, a walking miracle, an example that God hears and answers our prayers for healing today.

My deepest gratitude goes to my family and friends. My husband Marvin's love and counsel have been indispensable to me during the writing of these poems. Marvin also gets credit for leading me to my publisher, Xulon Press. My sincere appreciation goes to Libby Breeding for typing my original manuscript. Our son Scott, a Methodist pastor, and his lovely wife Ali, have been wonderful in their assistance in the preparation of my final manuscript. To our beautiful daughter Cathy, and dear friends Bill and Lynn Wagner, thank you for your constant support and encouragement.

My heartfelt thanks also go to my brother Bob Caldwell, his family, my sister Ruth Wright's family, and my cousin Elizabeth Rather for their love and appreciation of my poetry. The families of Marvin's brothers Ray and Kenneth Adkins, and his sister Chrysteen Campbell have offered their love and support. In honor of Jesus' birth, I write a Christmas poem each year. From those who receive it, I am most grateful for the many kind comments and notes encouraging me to publish. To everyone at Xulon Press, I extend my deepest thanks.

Be patient, remain hopeful and stand firm in your faith. Be encouraged by reading the Bible to pray and believe. Jesus said, "If thou canst believe, all things are possible to him that believeth" (Mark 9:23). Billy Graham, in his book, *The Secret of Happiness*, calls the King James Version of the Bible both "beautiful and beloved." I quote the King James in this book because I share Dr. Graham's affection for this translation. "…Not by might, nor by power, but by my spirit, saith the Lord of Hosts" (Zechariah 4:6). Through the Holy Spirit let us offer prayers of faith for the miracles within God's will today.

Barbara C. Adkins, Louisville, TN
July, 2006

Foreword

Reading the poems from the heart, mind, and pen of Barbara Caldwell Adkins is an inspiration to me. She writes about things that really matter in life—and she gives us hope and inspiration.

Her poems tell us of God's gift of healing and that God gives us life and joy. Her poems open our minds wider to the fact that the key to receiving God's blessings is believing and that Jesus, God's Son, can overcome evil.

These poems make very clear miracles that are recorded in the four gospels of the New Testament, and gives understanding and inspiration. We are blessed as we read again of God's conquering love, and His power to bless our lives and meet our needs.

These poems assure us of the friend we have in Jesus, and how the hunger of both our body and our heart can be met.

It blesses us to be reassured that God is a Father, Son, and Holy Spirit.

Barbara Caldwell Adkins' poems are inspired by the miracles of our Lord and reading them gives us inspiration and assurance. It is wonderful that Barbara could so beautifully express the truths that Jesus demonstrated through His miracles.

Charles L. Allen

Rise and Be Healed

With the rising of the sun
The work of miracles is begun.
Through the power in Jesus' blood
Comes a mighty healing flood.

With the glow of each sunrise
God sees us with holy eyes.
Through Jesus, The Light of the World, we may
Rise and be healed today.

With the warmth that sunbeams bring,
God's love flows through everything.
He gives us love, life and Spring.
Rise, be healed and sing!

With the setting of the sun
All fear is gone; the victory won.
Our souls, freed from strife,
Rise to eternal life.

This poem is a tribute to my dear friend, Bill Wagner, who gave me the title for this book. Bill Wagner has been in ministry over 30 years as a gospel singer, song writer, evangelist, and missionary.

Without You Nothing We Can Do

Lord, Your Word tells of miracles—
I love them all.
It is because you believe
And hear My call.

Thank You, Lord, use me—
Thy will be mine.
You are a branch,
I am the vine.*

To be Your branch
Brings much love to mind.
It rises within—
You are caring and kind.

It is because I care I pray—
Thy will be done.
Never cease to trust Me—
Jesus, God's Son.

Lord, without You
*Nothing we can do.**
The truth is yours—
My love is, too.

The truth is love—
It sets us free.
My Word is truth—
Read more of Me.

What is it, Lord,
We are to see?
How to bring
More souls to Me.

Open the windows
Of Heaven wide!
It is with joy—
I am by your side!

*"I am the vine, ye are the branches: He that abideth in me and I in him, the same bringeth forth much fruit: for without me ye can do nothing." John 15:5

Without Compromise

Lord, Your first miracle
Was at a wedding feast.[1]
The disciples truly believed—
Not one doubted in the least.

My Father's glory shone forth
As the Governor tasted the wine.
He said the best was saved until last—
Six stone waterpots touched by the Divine.

Each waterpot was filled to the brim
With water You said to draw.
Then the miraculous happened—
As Your disciples saw.

They saw the water turn to wine
Before their very eyes.
Blessed are your eyes because you believe
Without compromise.

Thy Son Liveth

Lord, You were in Cana of Galilee
When the nobleman came to call.[2]
He asked You to heal his son
Of a high fever which would not fall.

This man firmly believed
In My Father's power, strong to heal.
I said, "Thy son liveth"
Because his faith was real.

Lord, help us have real faith
As we walk with You today.
To know "Thy son liveth"
Before word comes, as we pray.

The nobleman was not surprised—
Before his servants spoke, he knew.
The fever left him at the seventh hour—
These words confirmed what was true.

To Love and Understand

Lord, in Simon's boat, sitting,
You taught the people on the shore.[3]
If I could have heard Your words,
I would have longed for more.

I know you are hungry
To feed upon My Word.
Believe that I am with you—
I will bless you by what you've heard.

Lord, Simon was blessed;
Yet, he said for You to depart
Because he was a sinful man.
Instead, he received Your heart.

Please clearly see I come
To fill your need.
Simon toiled with no success—
I was there to lead.

Master, forever be with me—
I long to be with You.
Search deeply within me—
Fill my mind with words anew.

You are My disciple today—
Simon was long ago.
Because you humbly believe,
The words I send, you'll know.

Lord, Simon, James and John
Forsook all and followed You.
I give You, my life,
My treasure, and my heart, too.

Barbara, you are brave and bold
To reach out and take My hand.
Never doubt My promise to you:
To love and understand.

Simply, Hold My Hand

Lord, Your Holy Spirit is within me—
I sense Your presence near.
It is with joy I pen Your words—
Words so very dear.

Your fourth miracle is a comfort.
It tells of Your command
For an unclean spirit
To depart from a certain man.[4]

You say this is a comfort.
I understand why.
An unclean spirit is causing evil
Through one he occupies.

Yes, Lord, we need You
To act today.
Please cast out the demons
As I fast and pray.

You are heeding My instruction
Made clear when I was on earth.
Prayer and fasting are required
To give certain miracles birth.

Thank You, Lord, for this knowledge.
It is a privilege to serve You.
Please let my humble offering
Reflect this miracle true.

The love that surrounds you
Is powerful indeed.
You are willing to be used
To help another in great need.

Yes, Lord, I am willing–
Please help me to understand
Exactly what I am to do.
Simply, hold My hand.*

*"For I the Lord thy God will hold thy right hand, saying unto thee, Fear not; I will help thee." Isaiah 41:13.

The Promise

Jesus passed through an angry mob[5]
Ready to cast Him down the hill.
They had led Him there
With plans that could kill.

How did He walk away
When He was well hemmed in?
Read of the promise in Psalms:*
There's a mighty protection from sinful men.

Marvin also escaped the bullets
Shot by a murderer, who was mystified–
How could he have missed Marvin,
When all others, he robbed, had died?

Marvin believes in angels,
God's messengers and guardians, dear.
Without a doubt, they were with him,
As with Jesus, it is very clear.

*"He shall give his angels charge over thee, to keep thee in all thy ways." Psalm 91:11

On the night before Thanksgiving 1995, my husband, Marvin, was attacked and robbed as he was coming home. Our daughter, Cathy, and I watched as a gunman unloaded his gun at Marvin at point blank range; the other robber then began hitting him with a stick. By God's grace Marvin escaped without serious injury. I spent that next day, Thanksgiving, thanking God for sparing Marvin.

Miracles Lie Around You

Lord, as You looked upon her,[6]
Love came beaming from Your eyes.
Then the fever vanished
Which came as no surprise.

The room was quiet—
I sent everyone away.
She was very ill—
On her death bed, she lay.

It was with love and compassion,
I took her hand in Mine.
She arose immediately,
And ministered to thine.

Lord, I can well imagine
The gladness and the tears.
A grand celebration—
To remember through the years!

Please touch our lives
With repeated joy today.
Send Your Spirit, through us,
To heal as we pray.

Believe this is possible,
And so it will be.
Miracles lie around you,
Waiting, to set others free.

continued

Lord, I am praying.
You must lead and guide.
I can do nothing,
Without You, by my side.

Yes, but with Me,
Everything you can do.
Go forth, unafraid—
I shall be with you.

The Rainbow

Jesus simply touched him,
And spoke the Word:
"Thou be clean. . ." *and* ". . . go before the priest."[7]
The leper was healed, as others heard.

Others heard about the miracle
Through the man that was healed.
Jesus asked that he tell no one;
Yet, he refused his lips be sealed.

If we ask for a miracle,
The Master to touch a life,
We should stand ready
To make any sacrifice.

The sacrifice of praise and worship
Is never hard.
We must trust Jesus!
He will lead and guard.

To lead us from temptation,
To guard our lives from pain,
To give us hope and encouragement,
Like the rainbow that follows rain.

Sickness, disappointment and evil
Lurk around us every day.
Yet, they do not have to bind us;
If, faithfully, we pray.

continued

Pray for the miracles
Which you long to see.
Refuse to become discouraged,
With Jesus comes victory!

Seek and find the Master,
Bow down on bended knee.
My Spirit comes, like the rainbow,*
To love and comfort thee.

* ". . and there was a rainbow round about the throne, in sight like unto an emerald." Revelation 4:30

Please, With Healing Descend

The four men had courage and strength;
But, their faith was the key.
They lowered their friend
For Jesus to see.[8]

The Master saw quickly
There was a great need.
He said, "Thy sins are forgiven;"
Yet, some disbelieved.

Little did they understand
That Jesus was God's Son.
When He healed the man,
A victory was won!

"Victory in Jesus"
Let us triumphantly sing!
Believing and rejoicing,
Let our praises ring!

Jesus, our Saviour,
And Lord of mankind,
Comes to perform miracles
When faith fills your mind.

In faith and in love,
I pray for Linda, my friend.
Lord, you know her needs—
*Please, with healing descend.**

continued

You know how she is lifted
And lowered to her chair.
Please let her walk–
This is my prayer.

My prayer is in flight
To our Father in Heaven,
On thankful wings for healing,
And, forgiveness, seventy times seven.

*"But they that wait upon the Lord; shall renew their strength; they shall mount up with wings as eagles; they shall run and not be weary; and they shall walk, and not faint." Isaiah 40:31.

Linda Harless had a beautiful smile that radiated her love for the Lord and others. She was a wonderful mother, teacher and friend; who, after brain surgery, taught herself to play the piano again. Linda graciously played the piano at Alcoa First Methodist Church and Fairpark Healthcare Center. Even when she had to be pushed in her wheelchair to the piano, she loved to play and sing "Holy, Holy, Holy". Linda now sings in Heaven's angel choir as her perfect healing came through death on January l, 2001.

The Gospel Must Be Heard

The sacred Scriptures tell us
Of an angel sent from God.
He troubled the waters in a pool at Bethesda
Where the lame and sick did nod.

Someone else always reached the water,
To be healed, before an impotent man.
For thirty and eight years, he was hopeful
With a faith that said, "I can."

"I can be healed" was in his heart—
A belief, so strong and true.
The Master came saying, "Arise and walk,"[9]
Which this man was thrilled to do!

Faith that moves a mountain,
And faith that heals the sick,
Is faith that keeps on believing
When results we don't see quick.

Someone else may move faster.
Someone else may step ahead.
Remember the Lord is watching
To see by whom we're led.

Those led by heavenly forces
Know it's their faith that counts.
If we are persistent,
Our inner strength just mounts.

continued

The Lord is ever with us—
He promised never would He leave.
His Holy Ghost is our helper,
If only we believe.

Believe and strongly witness!
Proclaim the sacred Word!
Refuse to sit in silence!
The Gospel must be heard!

The Greatest Gift

Lord, when I think of our hands–
I simply say "thank You."
Beautiful hands given to us
To use in service true.

With love and compassion, You looked
At the man with the withered hand.[10]
As he stood forth, my heart, as Yours,
Would have gone out to understand.

How could some of those present
Harden their hearts with no care?
This grieved and angered You, Lord.
They were wrong to stand in judgment there.

Hardness of heart is found today—
Some will judge and ridicule you.
Be bold and mighty forces will come to aid—
Stand firm and believe what is true.

Lord, I know the truth
Only You can heal today.
I say boldly, "I believe"
In mighty forces that come my way.

Whose hands are withered
That you know?
Withered because in service
They refuse to go.

continued

Lord, for him I'm praying long—
Please heal him and his hardened heart.
May Your birthday open the door—
He knows You are ready to do Your part.

Your part is to forgive and pray—
In love and compassion live.
Wholeness will come to him.
Love is the greatest gift you give.

Centurion Faith

Lord, my heart is touched deeply
By the quiet and wonderful way,
You healed the centurion's servant,[11]
As You walked along that day.

You received a message
About the servant who was very ill.
You did not go to him in person—
You simply did our Father's will.

Reading of this mighty healing
Gives me every reason to believe:
You are carefully listening to us.
All doubts, You will relieve.

Give us centurion faith, Lord,
To ask for healing of others, dear.
*May we pray with great confidence**
*Knowing, You are very near.***

* "Cast not away therefore your confidence, which hath great recompence of reward." Hebrews 10:35

** "But without faith *it is* impossible to please *him*; for he that cometh to God must believe that he is, and *that* he is a rewarder of them that diligently seek him." Hebrews 11:6

Your Walk On Earth Into Eternity

Lord, You saw the widowed mother
At the gate of the city Nain.[12]
Her only son was carried out—
She was in much grief and pain.

I can well imagine
The love and compassion in Your eyes,
As You said, "Weep not," *to her,*
And "Young man, I say unto thee, Arise."

Your hand was on his coffin
As he sat up and began to speak.
The people declared You a great prophet,
And glorified God, week by week.

Two of John's disciples
Were sent to question You:
"Art thou He that should come?"
Or, was there to be another true?

In the very same hour
You made the blind to see
And the lame to walk—
All there, to believe.

Your miracles are our living proof
Of Your divinity.
Thank You for Your walk
On earth into eternity.

Lord, You rule my spirit
As Your Spirit makes me whole.
Thank You, Lord Jesus, my Saviour,
For saving my very soul.

You are touching the very heart of Me.
Never fear death as you are part of Me.
I will love and cherish you
For all eternity.

We're Marching To Zion

We know even the devils
Are obedient to our Lord.
The devil, blind and dumb,
Was removed by the Sword.[13]

The finger of God cast out
The devil from a man,
Who saw and spake,
As the devil ran.

The people were amazed—
Some disbelieved.
Did Beelzebub,
Chief of the devils, succeed?

Jesus said Satan's kingdom
Would never stand
If the devils were cast out
By Beelzebub's hand.

Jesus taught other lessons
As He spoke that day.
He said a house divided,
Against a house, falleth in the way.

Every kingdom divided against itself
Will be brought to desolation.
So let us be aware of
Every temptation.

The devil is ever present—
Prowling, like a lion.
Trying to deceive us—
As we're marching to Zion.

We must be united.
We must hear Your call.
We must remain loyal.
We must refuse to fall.

Peace, Be Still

Lord, grant us the peace we seek.
Through You, our prayers ascend.
Thank You for those who touch us—
Thank You for each friend.

Your friends are loyal.
Those that I send
Will stand by you forever—
Days, without end.

Lord, we know this is true—
Those dearest, and closest, are few.
In every case, we know them
Because they come from You.

The bond you have with My own
Is a bond of purest gold.
The reason is simple—
Their faith in Me is bold.

Bill's faith in You is bold.
He has walked, where You walked
By the Sea of Galilee—
He has talked, where You talked.

Bill is My own.
I love him dear.
My presence is with him—
I am always near.

Lord, it touched my heart
As Bill talked of preaching,
And standing by the sea,
Where You stood teaching.

The beauty of the water
Is beyond compare.
My presence lingers
In the air.

Bill spoke of the acoustics
Because of the hills that surround.
He said they create
Wonderful sound.

The words that I spoke,
He is speaking today.
To lead others to Me,
He points the way.

Thank You, Lord, for leading—
The way making clear.
Thank You for calming the sea,
And, within us, all fear.

I calm the wind, and
To the waves, I say, "Peace, be still."[14]
Within you, I quieten the tempest—
Your soul, with peace, I fill.

This poem is a tribute to my many dear Christian friends. Bill Wagner's stories of his trips to the Holy Land greatly helped me to write this poem.

Through My Gates, Enter In

"Go!" *spoke our Lord*
To many devils in Legion, a man.[15]
The command sent them into 2,000 swine,
Which drown, as they violently ran.

The unclean devils are fierce
As they gain control.
Man must remain in My Spirit
Who serves to patrol.

Are You saying without You,
We are likely to fall?
To be devoured by devils,
If we don't heed Your call?

Yes, be aware of temptations—
Satan attacks you when weak.
The story of Legion
Tells you whom you must seek.

Thank You, Lord Jesus,
We seek You, alone.
Fill us with confidence
As we approach Your throne.

Come boldly forward
With songs filled with praise.
Great love and thanksgiving
To our Father, please raise.

Lord, we sing praises most gladly
As humbly we come.
Forgiving others their sins,
Seventy times seven, for some.

You know what's required—
Through My gates, enter in!
My love fills and protects
As I pardon your sin.

The River To Your Soul

The river to Legion's soul
Was flooded with waters deep
In a multitude of devils–
Legion's soul to keep.

Only Jesus was unafraid.
The devils begged to be sent
Into the herd of swine–
To a quick death they went.[16]

Devils are captive
In the river to the soul,
In many whom Jesus
Longs to make whole.

The devils of death
Lead souls into hell.
Jesus, and His angels,
Lead you to Heaven, to dwell.

The devils are bound
In each one they enter;
Unless, in Jesus' name,
We command their surrender.

No devil can exist
In a heart full of love,
Which welcomes God's power,
That comes from above.

The river to your soul
Is wide and deep.
With love and commitment,
God will safely keep.

Flood the river with waters
Deep in God's Word.
My Spirit transforms you
As the Gospel is heard.

The Gift of Healing

Lord, the woman in the crowd
Was desperate as she came.
When she touched Your garment,
She was never again the same.[17]

Because of her faith in Me,
I declared her whole.
The bleeding stopped immediately—
She loved Me with her soul.

Your Word says with fear and trembling,
Before You, she fell.
Telling everyone why she touched You,
And how You made her well.

Can you imagine
How you would feel
If for twelve years, you were bleeding,
And no physician could heal?

Yes, Lord, I can imagine—
I'm so thankful You were there.
This miracle tells me
Your healing power was in the air.

In the air that surrounds you,
My power is increasing now.
The gift of healing is yours
As humbly, you bow.

Lord, it is my hands—
I know Your power is there.
Lead me to use it,
To our Father's glory, is my prayer.

You will be used—
I will prepare the way.
You will give My comfort,
My peace, to others, as you pray.

Resurrection Faith

Unto Jairus, ruler of the synagogue,
You said, "Be not afraid. Only believe."[18]
Jairus thought his daughter dead.
His greatest fear, You did relieve.

It was My joy
To take her hand,
To see her face,
And watch her stand.

Thank You, Lord.
Deep love You showed
For a girl of twelve,
With face that glowed.

Jairus knew his daughter,
I could save.
Because of his faith,
New life I gave.

New life for a daughter
And the widow's son.
Do not fear death—
The victory is won.

Yes, Lord, they saw the victory—
As did You.
Thank You for words of assurance,
Which I know are true.

Lord, why these mighty miracles
Of long ago?
So, resurrection faith
You would know.

I love You, Lord Jesus.
Humbly, I bow.
Thank You for resurrection faith—
Growing stronger now.

With His Stripes We Are Healed

Lord, thank You for giving
The two blind men their vision.[19]
You touched their eyes
Because they met Your provision.

No miracle is performed
Through unbelievers.
The men had faith in Me—
They became receivers.

They received sight;
The miracle called seeing.
They beheld My light;
The miracle called believing.

It is with divine joy
That I restore sight.
Truly, you can transcend
From darkness to light.

Lord, this is a great truth
For those blind today.
May Your awesome power
Descend upon others, I pray.

The key is believing.
In your faith, firmly stand.
If symptoms tarry,
Still praise God's mighty hand.

Forget about feelings—
Proclaim God's Holy Word!
Healing will come to those
Who claim what they've heard.

Honor My words
On sacred pages:
"With His stripes we are healed,"*
Rings through the ages!

*"But he was wounded for our transgressions, he was bruised for our iniquities: the chastisement of our peace was upon him; and with his stripes we are healed." Isaiah 53:5

The Truth

How could a dumb man
Suddenly speak?
Jesus cast out the devil[20]
That made the man weak.

The multitudes marveled,
But some disbelieved.
The Pharisees said
The prince of the devils relieved.

How do we know
This miracle was done
By Jesus,
God's son?

I told you before.
The truth does not lie.
If the prince cast out his devils,
His kingdom would die.

Breaking The Bread

Lord, Your love for the people
Led You to feed them all.
You looked up to Heaven,
Blessing five loaves, and two fishes, small.[21]

Five thousand men,
Beside women and children all,
Were fed as the bread was broken
Because our Father heard My call.

Your call produced a feast—
Heaven's door was opened wide.
The people were fed with joy,
By the disciples at Your side.

The bread and meat were so abundant
Everyone ate until satisfied,
With twelve baskets remaining
Of fragments, which were denied.

God will honor your prayer of faith—
His power is great indeed
When you pray to our Father,
In My name, with your need.

You are rightly praying—
I hear your earnest pleas.
You feed My lambs and sheep
As you fall upon your knees.

continued

Lord, I lead Your children
*To thank You for their bread.**
They are fed and nourished
By the very words they've said.

I hear their tender voices.
My lambs are in your care.
They open Heaven's door
With precious words of prayer.

* "But Jesus called them *unto him* and said, 'Suffer little children to come unto me, and forbid them not: for of such is the kingdom of God.'" Luke 18:16

Love Conquers All

Lord, love moved You across the water
As You walked upon the sea.[22]
Your disciples were afraid
Until You brought security.

"Be of good cheer; it is I;
Be not afraid," *You spoke.*
Their eyes thought You a spirit.
Their ears, You awoke.

"Come," *You said to Peter*
As he walked upon the sea.
Then You reached out and saved him
When the winds blew boisterously.

Peter's feet were sinking
As fear engulfed his soul.
His faith failed to sustain him;
So, in love, You took control.

Today, we are like Peter
When the storms of life we face.
Fear takes us captive
When faith we should embrace.

Can we not simply remember:
You are as close as the air we breathe?
You have promised You will save us—
All our fears to relieve.

continued

Lord, let us, like Your disciples,
Listen to Your gentle call.
Help us to be cheerful,
Encouraging to all.

This is a great lesson.
Be of strong faith and recall.
God's love reigns eternal—
Love conquers all.

Enlightenment

Lord, thank You for enlightenment
Given unto me.
I know, without a doubt,
Again, You calmed the sea.[23]

I can see Your disciples
Standing there in awe.
When the storm ceased–
Land, immediately, they saw.

Such rapid change happens
Only through Your powers.
Had the disciples rowed to shore,
It could have taken hours.

You are rightly understanding
My power to intercede.
I come instantly
When great is the need.

Lord, I well remember.
I know that this is so.
You moved my car–
So to death, I did not go.

It was the same
Upon the sea.
You believe, as My disciples,
And are very precious to Me.

continued

Truly, Lord, I praise You
And bless Your holy name.
Please enlighten more of Your children
So they will worship You, the same.

My angels are rejoicing!
Totally lost sheep are some
Who will be headed homeward—
With enlightenment, they will come!*

*"I say unto you, that likewise joy shall be in heaven over one sinner that repenteth, more than over ninety and nine just persons, which need no repentance." Luke 15:7

Several years ago I was driving on Alcoa Highway in the left hand lane close to the Knoxville Airport. Suddenly, a tremendous truck pulled out in front of my car. It appeared to be an unavoidable collision. I turned my steering wheel to the right, and, immediately, my car, as straight as an arrow, was passing the truck. It was an awesome moment knowing God had saved me.

With Authority

Lord Jesus, because she cried after them,
Your disciples were distressed–
Asking You to send the mother away.
Instead, the problem You addressed.[24]

The love she had for her daughter
Shone as she fell at My feet.
Yet, to cast the children's bread
To the dogs, I said was not meet.

She said, "Truth, Lord: yet, of the crumbs
Which fall from their masters' table, the dogs eat."
I made her daughter whole from that hour.
Her great faith prevented defeat.

Lord, I thank You
And praise You now.
In the greatness of Your presence,
Humbly, I bow.

I believe in Your power
With my heart, mind and soul,
To cast out all devils,
As You take control.

You are rightly sensing
My power is as real today
As when on earth
I knelt to pray.

continued

*Lord, I speak boldly to the devils**
Within one today,
Who is grievously vexed,
And has lost his way.

You must speak with authority
Knowing My words are true.
Satan will flee, when cast out,
In My name, by you.**

*"Behold, I give unto you power . . . over all the power of the enemy: and nothing shall by any means hurt you." Luke 10:19

**"Notwithstanding in this rejoice not, that the spirits are subject unto you; but rather rejoice, because your names are written in heaven." Luke 10:20

I Am Jesus, Your Friend

Lord, Your many miracles
Performed here on earth,
Make me ponder their purpose.
Was it to give other miracles birth?

Yes, please recall My words:
Greater works you shall do.*
I ascended to My Father
To make these words come true.

Lord, You opened deaf ears and
Clear speech You gave.[25]
Please use us, Lord Jesus,
The afflicted to save.

Lord, You know who it is
That needs You, today.
Lead us unto them—
Give us the right words to say.

You, I am leading
With great joy in My heart.
You will know whom I have chosen—
My power to impart.

Thank You for words
Of assurance today.
It is with great honor
I pen the words which You say.

continued

Lord, may Your power
Descend from You on high.
Please perform miracles through us
Because on You, we rely.

I am your Saviour—
With great love, I descend.
To you, through My Spirit,
I am Jesus, your Friend.**

*"Verily, verily, I say unto you, He that believeth on me, the *works that* I do shall he do also; and greater works than these shall he do; because I go unto my Father." John 14:12

**"Greater love hath no man than this, that a man lay down his life for his friends." John 15:13

Through Your Mighty Power

Lord, with compassion for them,
After three days of fasting,
You would not send them away
Without strength that was lasting.[26]

The multitude sat on the ground
As I blessed the bread.
I broke seven loaves.
About four thousand were fed.

Then, Lord, You blessed
A few fishes small.
You broke them,
Providing enough for all.

My disciples collected fragments
Of meat which remained.
Seven baskets were filled
As the Scriptures explained.

The people were hungry.
You fed them that hour.
They were satisfied
Through Your mighty power.

Lord, for three days,
You led me to pray and fast.
Through Your mighty power,
You saved a life to last.

continued

Are three days as long
As a fast needs to be?
You understand
What is required of thee.

After three days, Lord,
You arose from the dead.
Through Your mighty power,
We arise and are led.

Your Holy Spirit Send

Lord Jesus, I praise You.
I thank God for keen vision.
Daily, as I open my eyes,
And see with great precision.

In Bethsaida, a man besought You
His vision to restore.[27]
He believed You could help him
To bring sight once more.

Then, You spit and touched his eyes.
He saw men as trees, walking.
When You touched his eyes, again,
He saw, clearly, as You were talking.

Lord, please today, Your Holy Spirit send
Others' vision to restore.
Lead me, Lord, my hands to lay
*On eyes, to see, once more.**

* "But we have this treasure in earthen vessels, that the excellency of the power may be of God, and not of us." II Corinthians 4:7

I Am Jesus, The Good Shepherd

Nothing shall be impossible
*The sacred Scriptures teach.**
With God, we know the good
Lies within our reach.

Lord, give us patience
Within ourselves to know,
When things look the bleakest
To You, we must go.

The distressed father came unto You,
Because his son, a lunatic,
Was possessed by an unclean spirit,
Quick to torment and make sick.[28]

He wallowed on the ground, foaming,
And into the fire he fell.
Then, often into water,
He was thrown, as well.

The father said this spirit
Was trying to destroy his son.
He asked You for help and compassion,
So victory would be won.

You told the father:
"If thou canst believe,
Everything is possible. . ."
The believer will receive.

The father cried out:
"Lord, I believe. . ."
Begging for help
So, he would receive.

Lord, You commanded
The unclean spirit leave.
You said ". . . no more enter him."
All fear, You did relieve.

As the spirit left him
To the ground he was thrown.
Many thought him dead
Until raised by Your hand, alone.

The disciples asked why
This spirit they could not cast out.
You explained prayer and fasting
Were the necessary route.

Lord, today, we know
The same truths apply.
That is why on You, only,
We completely rely.

As you enter My pasture
You, I will feed.
I am Jesus, The Good Shepherd**—
Forever, I will lead.

* "For with God nothing shall be impossible." Luke 1:37

**"I am the good shepherd, and know my sheep, and am known of mine." John 10:14

My Treasury

Lord, why in a fish's mouth
Would tribute money be?[29]
You sent Peter to cast a hook
Down by the sea.

Peter was a fisherman
Before he followed Me.
Where else would I send him?
The fish held My treasury.

Lord, You said from the fish,
Caught first, he would find
A piece of money—
The exact amount and kind.

Yes, I provided
Money for the need.
Think of how I do the same
Now, as you, I lead.

For Judgment

Your will be done, Father,
As when Jesus was on earth.
Through Your Spirit, sight came
To a man, blind since birth.[30]

Lord, You spat on the ground,
And from the spittle made clay.
His eyes You anointed, and said,
"Go, wash in the pool of Siloam" *that day.*

The blind man went his way,
Washed, and came seeing.
Some said, "This is he."
Others, "It is like him," disbelieving.

But he said, "I am he."
"How were thine eyes opened?" they asked.
He said Jesus anointed his eyes—
He washed to complete the task.

Many Pharisees and Jews refused to believe—
They cast the man out.
Then Jesus found him,
And offered him another route.

Jesus asked the man if
He believed on the Son of God.
The man wanted to know who He was,
So "Yes," he could nod.

continued

"Thou hast both seen Him,
And it is He that talketh with thee," *Jesus said.*
The man spoke, "I believe."
To worship, he was led.

For judgment, Jesus said
He came into the world so the blind might see.
He also said others who see
Will become blind because of sin that be.

All Things Are Possible

Lord, You gave the warning—
You made it very clear.
You said those not with You
Are against You and scattereth near.

Scattereth because one gathereth not;
No stand is made for You.
The evil spirit leaves and returns
With seven other spirits, more evil, too.[31]

So, the last state of a man
Is worse than the first, by far.
He allowed the evil spirits
His life to deeply mar.

Lord, I stand upon Your Word.
Firmly, I believe.
*With You all things are possible.**
I pray, his soul, You will still receive.

*"Jesus said unto him, 'If thou canst believe, all things are possible to him that believeth.'" Mark 9:23

The Key

Lord, for 18 years You said
Satan had her bound.[32]
Her healing was rapid
Once I was found.

Lord, I know
Finding You is the key.
Without Me, defeating Satan is
An impossibility.

Lord, Satan is a liar.
He told her that she could not stand.
Yet, you see what happened
When she took My hand.

Lord, help us hasten
Your hand to quickly hold.
I will unlock Heaven's treasures:
Health and happiness of purest gold.

The Logic

Lord, You raised the question:
"Is it lawful to heal on the sabbath day?"
Those present held their peace.
Nothing could they say.

The man who had the dropsy—
You took and healed that day.[33]
I laid My hands upon him.
Healing comes as I pray.

You asked who would let
His ass or ox fall into a pit,
And not straightway pull it out?
Lord, I could not watch and sit.

Those present could not
Answer Me a word.
They understood the logic
In the words they heard.

The Thanks You Should Give

Why, Lord, to the priests
Did, You, the ten lepers send?[34]
To thank God for healing—
To thank Me, Jesus, their Friend.

Your Word states:
They were cleansed as they went.
The Samaritan glorified God for his healing.
This stranger gave thanks sincerely meant.

You asked, "Were not ten cleansed
But where are the nine?"
They thought of themselves only—
They gave no thankful sign.

The grateful one was rewarded—
You said, "Thy faith hath made thee whole."
He was very humble—
He loved Me with his soul.

Lord, I know being thankful
Is a vital part.
Continue always to thank Me—
Speak to Me from your heart.

Lord, help us teach children
To be thankful today.
It brings Me great joy
To hear them as they pray.

Lord, I know You are reached
By thanksgiving and by praise.
You know the importance of using
The hands that you raise.

By Your words and example,
We know how to live.
Remember always
The thanks you should give.

Your Eyes I Will Open

Mary and Martha were in sorrow.
I can imagine their depth of pain.
If death should take my brother,
Tears would fall like heavy rain.

Lord, guard Bob, my brother—
Protect him, day by day.
Precious is he to us—
Grant him long life, I pray.

Mary and Martha sent for You, Lord,
Saying, ". . . he whom thou lovest is sick."[35]
You said, "This sickness is . . . for the glory of God."
Two more days You abode, rather than going quick.

You told Your disciples,
"Our friend Lazarus sleepeth."
They thought You spoke of taking rest—
Then, "Lazarus is dead," *plainly, You speaketh.*

As You traveled to Bethany,
Martha met You in the way.
You told her Lazarus would rise again.
She thought You meant the last day.

"I am the resurrection, and the life:
He that believeth in Me, though he were dead,
Yet he shall live."
These eternal words, You said.

"And whosoever liveth and
Believeth in Me shall never die.
Believest thou this?"
Lord, I could never deny.

*"I believe thou art the Christ,
The Son of God that should come . . ."
These eloquent words of Martha
Were followed by tears from some.*

*Mary, and the Jews that were with her,
Were weeping as to You, they came.
You were troubled, and groaned in spirit–
You wept, as they did the same.*

*Lord, then You groaned again–
As to the grave You went.*
"Take ye away the stone"
Was the command, You sent.

"Lazarus come forth!"
*In a loud voice, You cried.
The mighty miracle happened–
Lazarus opened his eyes!*

Your eyes I will open
On your resurrection day.
All the splendors of Heaven
Await believers who pray.

His Vision, I Awoke

Lord, You heard the blind beggar
And commanded he be brought to You.[36]
He was very humble and
Asked for mercy, true.

"Jesus, thou Son of David,
Have mercy on me."
His words touched My heart.
His face I had to see.

Lord, You asked him plainly
What he desired of Thee.
That his eyes be opened—
To receive his sight from Me.

"Receive thy sight:
Thy faith hath saved thee," *You spoke.*
Immediately, he saw.
His vision, I awoke.

Open Wide The Door

To blind Bartimaeus, You spoke:
"Go thy way, thy faith hath made thee whole."[37]
Bartimaeus loved Me
With his heart, mind and soul.

Bartimaeus followed You, Lord:
A witness to Your glory.
He holds a place of honor
In the Gospel story.

You gave him sight, Lord–
A priceless gift to treasure.
His faith in Me is real–
Far beyond measure.

Our faith is real, Lord–
Give us eyes that truly see.
Open wide the door– *
I will come to thee.

*"Behold, I stand at the door, and knock: if any man hear my voice, and open the door, I will come in to him, and will sup with him, and he with me." Revelation 3:20.

Pray, Firmly Believing

Lord, the fig tree withered
Because firmly You believed.
No fruit would grace its branches—
Your command, it received.[38]

*Help us pray, firmly believing—**
Refusing all doubts that come to mind.
Strengthen us, Lord, our fears relieving,
To voice prayers of the proper kind.

I know all things are possible
*As we pray to our Father in Your name.***
I command the demons leave
With their lies and their shame.

So, in faith, with nothing doubting,
Father, I pray Your will be done.
Mold us to Your likeness:
A reflection of Jesus, Your precious Son.

*"And all things, whatsoever ye shall ask in prayer, believing, ye shall receive." Matthew 21:22.

**"And in that day ye shall ask me nothing. Verily, verily, I say unto you, Whatsoever ye shall ask the Father in my name, he will give *it* you." John 16:23.

The Power Of The Holy Spirit

Lord, Judas knew the place
Where You would be.[39]
He brought officers with him
To arrest Me.

With lanterns, torches and weapons
In the night they came.
I told them,
Jesus is My name.

Why, Lord, did those sent to apprehend You
Backward fall?
The power of the Holy Spirit
Overcame them all.

Lord, why did You not
Simply walk away?
It was My Father's will
That I should stay.

A Lesson In Compassion

Lord, Malchus took You captive;
Yet, to him, You were kind.
He was following orders—
No cruelty was in his mind.

Why, Lord, did Simon Peter
Cut off Malchus' ear?[40]
He was trying to defend Me.
His mind was full of fear.

Lord, You told Peter
To put his sword away.
I would drink My Father's cup.
It could be no other way.

Lord, Your Word says
You touched and healed Malchus' ear.
Great agony was in his face—
In his eyes many a tear.

Lord, this was Your last
Miracle of healing.
A great lesson in compassion
I was revealing.

Yes, Lord, we know.
Thank You for deeply caring.
It is you, I should thank.
My love, you are sharing.

With great joy I share
As love fills my heart.
Melody fills the air
As joy, you impart.

Your love lives within us.
Your sweet Spirit soars!
Trust Me always—
Love is opening many doors.

A Great Awakening

Lord, on the third day,
Why did You arise?[41]
There is a great awakening—
When dawn will grace your eyes.

It is through Your Holy Spirit,
I sense that this is so.
It is because you have fasted.
On the third day, you know.

On the third day comes renewal—
Your spirit awakes.
There is a transformation
Which your spirit makes.

It is a recreation.
You know God is very near.
He gives you new direction—
His timing is very clear.

Lord, why to Mary Magdalene
Did you first appear?
She understood My mission.
To her, I was very dear.

She thought You were the gardener,
With no idea You were near.
It was with great joy
I spoke her name, so dear.

Mary called You, "Rabonni"–
Meaning, Master, very dear.
She loved Me, deeply,
And wept many a tear.

By her, You sent us a precious message
As You stood on sacred sod:
". . . I ascend unto My Father, and your Father;
And to My God, and to your God."

Be My Disciples True

Lord, You said: "Cast your net
On the right side of the ship, and ye shall find."[42]
Your directions were exact,
Bringing encouragement to mind.

The disciples knew You
As the net was greatly filled.
The ship dragged the net to shore
Where it, at last, was stilled.

The net remained unbroken
As the fish were brought ashore.
Simon Peter drew the net,
One hundred and fifty-three, it bore.

"Come and dine," *You bade them—*
To eat fish and bread, You cooked.
It was because I loved them—
Hungry and tired, they looked.

Then, Lord, You spoke of love.
". . . lovest thou Me?" *three times, You asked.*
When you love, you become a servant—
Happy to do the simple task.

You spoke of feeding
Your lambs and Your sheep.
Those who love Me
Will My commandments keep.

Lord, let us hasten
Your commands to hear and know.
Listen carefully to Me—
I will direct you in My way to go.

With joy we will listen—
Through Your Spirit teach us now.
I will instruct you fully
As you pray and humbly bow.

Is there more, Lord?
What exactly are we to do?
Reach out to others—
Be My disciples true.*

Lord, help us witness boldly
*As we proclaim Your sacred Word.***
Others who are listening,
Are believing what they've heard.

Your Spirit, Lord, is moving—
Reaching across this great land.
Be prepared to travel—
Help others to understand.

Jesus, I lift my hands
*To praise and worship You.****
Thank you for being
My disciple true.

*"Then he called his twelve disciples together, and gave them power and authority over all devils, and to cure diseases." Luke 9:1

continued

**“And he sent them to preach the kingdom of God, and to heal the sick.” Luke 9:2

***“Lift up your hands in the sanctuary, and bless the Lord.” Psalm 134:2

Work Your Miracles In Great Array

The shadows of the evening
Bring thanksgiving for the day.
And for the working of miracles,
Lord, I thank You as I pray.

You deliver me from evil.
You protect me from all wrong.
You catch me when I am falling.
You lead me all day long.

Demons are made helpless.
It's impossible for them to stay
When boldly we command them: Go!
In Jesus' name this day!

What are you lacking?
Let your needs be known.
God will overflow your basket.
He cannot forget His own.

Never can God forget us.
We must always remember Him.
*One day He will judge us**
When our eyes are growing dim.

Do you fear death?
Forbid it to be so.
Remember those He raised up.
You, He, at death, will know.

continued

Many are in need of healing,
Anoint them with oil and pray.
"With His stripes we are healed."**
Rise and be healed today!

More miracles are needed.
Lord Jesus, in Your mighty way,
*You hear us calling for our loved ones,****
Work Your miracles in great array!

* "For we must all appear before the judgment seat of Christ; that every one may receive the things done in his body according to that he hath done, whether it be good or bad." II Corinthians 5:10

** ". . . and with his stripes we are healed." Isaiah 53:5

***"Thus saith the Lord, the Holy One of Israel, and his Maker, 'Ask me of things to come concerning my sons, and concerning the work of my hands command ye me.'" Isaiah 45:11

Appendices

THE MIRACLES OF OUR LORD[43]

MIRACLES OF SUPPLY

Water converted into wine
Peter's net filled with immense draught of fish
Five thousand men, besides women and children, fed
Four thousand men, besides women and children, fed
A fish furnishes tribute money
A great haul of fish

MIRACLES OF HEALING

Nobleman's son – of a fever
Peter's mother-in-law – of a fever
A man full of leprosy
A man borne by four – of palsy
The impotent man who had been afflicted thirty-eight years
The man with withered hand
The centurion's servant – of palsy
The woman who had been twelve years with issue of blood
Sight restored to two men
Hearing and speech restored to a man

Sight restored to a man
Sight given to a man who was born blind
A woman who had been eighteen years afflicted
A man – of dropsy
Ten men – of leprosy
Sight restored to a beggar
Sight restored to Bartimaeus
The ear of Malchus, the high priest's servant

MIRACLES OF EXORCISING DEVILS

The man of an unclean spirit
The demoniac who was blind and dumb
The two men possessed of Legion, exceeding fierce
The dumb man possessed of a devil
The daughter of the Syrophoenician woman
The lunatic boy, the disciples having failed
The devil that was dumb

MIRACLES OF JUDGMENT

The swine run down a steep place into the sea and are drowned
The fig tree withered

MIRACLES OF DELIVERANCE

He delivers Himself from His enemies
The wind and sea obey His word
Peter saved, trying to walk on the sea, as Jesus was walking
The wind ceases, and the vessel is instantly at the land
Those sent to apprehend Him fall backward

MIRACLES OF RAISING THE DEAD

The only son of a widow – as they were bearing him to the grave
The daughter of Jairus, the ruler of the synagogue
Lazarus – when he had been dead four days
His own body – the third day from interment

Endnotes

1. Miracle I. In the 27th Year of Our Lord, Water converted into wine. Cana. John 2:1-11.
2. Miracle II. In the 27th Year of Our Lord. Nobleman's son—of a fever. Cana. John 4:46-54.
3. Miracle III. In the 27th Year of Our Lord. Peter's net filled with immense draught of fish. Sea of Galilee. Luke 5:1-11.
4. Miracle IV. In the 27th Year of Our Lord. The man of an unclean spirit. Capernaum. Mark 1:23-26 and Luke 4:33-37.
5. Miracle V. In the 27th Year of Our Lord. Jesus delivers Himself from His enemies. Nazareth. Luke 4:30.
6. Miracle VI. In the 27th Year of Our Lord. Peter's mother-in-law of a fever. Capernaum. Matthew 8:14-17, Mark 1:29-31, and Luke 4:38-39.
7. Miracle VII. In the 27th Year of Our Lord. A man full of leprosy. Place near Chorazin. Matthew 8:2-4, Mark 1:40-45, and Luke 5:13-16.
8. Miracle VIII. In the 27th Year of Our Lord. The man borne by four – of palsy. Capernaum. Matthew 9:1-8, Mark 2:3-12, and Luke 5:17-26.
9. Miracle IX. In the 27th Year of Our Lord. The impotent man who was afflicted 38 years. Pool of Bethesda. John 5:1-16.

10. Miracle X. In the 27th Year of Our Lord. The man with withered hand. Capernaum. Matthew 12:9-13, Mark 3:1-5, and Luke 6:6-10.
11. Miracle XI. In the 27th Year of Our Lord. The centurion's servant of palsy. Capernaum. Matthew 8:5-13 and Mark 7:1-10.
12. Miracle XII. In the 27th Year of Our Lord. The only son of a widow—as they were bearing him to the grave. Nain. Luke 7:11-16.
13. Miracle XIII. In the 27th Year of Our Lord. The demoniac who was blind and dumb. Capernaum. Matthew 12:22-23, Mark 3:19-30, and Luke 11:14-23.
14. Miracle XIV. In the 27th Year of Our Lord. The wind and the sea obey His Word. Sea of Galilee. Matthew 8:23-37, Mark 4:37-41, and Luke 8:22-25.
15. Miracle XV. In the 27th Year of Our Lord. The two men possessed of Legion, exceeding fierce. Gadara. Matthew 8:28-34, Mark 5:1-20, and Luke 8:26-39.
16. Miracle XVI. In the 27th Year of Our Lord. The swine run down a steep place into the sea, and are drowned. Gadara. Matthew 8:30-32.
17. Miracle XVII. In the 27th Year of Our Lord. The woman who had been twelve years with issue of blood. Capernaum. Matthew 9:20-22, Mark 5:25-34, and Luke 8:43-48.
18. Miracle XVIII. In the 27th Year of Our Lord. The daughter of Jairus, ruler of the synagogue, raised from the dead. Capernaum. Matthew 9:18-26, Mark 5:22-43, and Luke 8:41-56.
19. Miracle XIX. In the 27th Year of Our Lord. Sight restored to two men in Capernaum. Matthew 9:27-31.
20. Miracle XX. In the 27th Year of Our Lord. The dumb man possessed of a devil at Capernaum. Matthew 9:32-35.
21. Miracle XXI. In the 28th Year of Our Lord. Five thousand men beside women and children fed. Decapolis.

Matthew 14:15-21, Mark 6:35-44, Luke 9:12-17, and John 6:5-14.

22. Miracle XXII. In the 28th Year of Our Lord. Peter saved, trying to walk on the sea, as Jesus was walking on the Sea of Galilee. Matthew 14:28-31 and Mark 6:45-52.
23. Miracle XXIII. In the 28th Year of Our Lord. The wind ceases, and the vessel is instantly at the land. The Sea of Galilee. Mark 6:51-52 and John 6:21.
24. Miracle XXIV. In the 28th Year of Our Lord. The daughter of the Syrophoenician woman at Borders of Tyre and Sidon. Matthew 15:21-28 and Mark 7:24-30.
25. Miracle XXV. In the 28th Year of Our Lord. Hearing and speech restored to a man. Decapolis. Mark 7:32-37.
26. Miracle XXVI. In the 28th Year of Our Lord. Four thousand men, besides women and children, fed at Decapolis. Matthew 15:32-39 and Mark 8:1-10.
27. Miracle XXVII. In the 28th Year of Our Lord. Sight restored to a man at Bethsaida. Mark 8:22-26.
28. Miracle XXVIII. In the 28th Year of Our Lord. The lunatic boy the disciples having failed. The Plain of Galilee. Matthew 17:14-21, Mark 9:14-30, and Luke 9:37-43.
29. Miracle XXIX. In the 28th Year of Our Lord. A fish furnishes tribute money. Sea of Galilee. Matthew 17:24-27.
30. Miracle XXX. In the 28th Year of Our Lord. Sight given to a man born blind. Pool of Siloam. John 9.
31. Miracle XXXI. In the 28th Year of our Lord. The devil that was dumb. Capernaum. Luke 11:14-26.
32. Miracle XXXII. In the 29th Year of Our Lord. A woman who had been 18 years afflicted. Galilee. Luke 13:11-17.
33. Miracle XXXIII. In the 29th Year of Our Lord.. A man of dropsy. Near Jerusalem. Luke 14:1-6.

34. Miracle XXXIV. In the 29th Year of Our Lord. Ten men of leprosy. Near Jerusalem. Luke 17:11-19.
35. Miracle XXXV. In the 29th Year of Our Lord. Lazarus—when he had been dead four days. Bethany. John 11:1-44.
36. Miracle XXXVI. In the 29th Year of Our Lord. Sight restored to a beggar. Jericho. Luke 18:35-43.
37. Miracle XXXVII. In the 29th Year of Our Lord. Sight restored to Bartimaeus. Jericho. Mark 10:46-52.
38. Miracle XXXVIII. In the 29th year of Our Lord. The fig tree withered. Near Bethany. Matthew 21:18-21 and Mark 11:12-14.
39. Miracle XXXIX. In the 29th Year of Our Lord. Those sent to apprehend Him fall backward. A garden over the brook Cedron. John 18:4-6.
40. Miracle XL. In the 29th Year of Our Lord. The ear of Malchus, the high priest's servant. A garden over the brook of Cedron. Luke 22:50-51.
41. Miracle XLI. In the 29th Year of Our Lord. His own body—the third day from interment. Garden of Joseph. Mark 16:9-11, Luke 24:1-7, and John 20:1-18.
42. Miracle XLII. In the 29th Year of Our Lord. A great haul of fish. Sea of Galilee. John 21:5-17.
43. *The Indexed Bible*, Copyright 1902, Jno. A. Dickson Publishing Co., Evansville, Indiana.

My Personal *Rise and Be Healed* Prayer Journal

Printed in the United States
63669LVS00002BA/1-249

9 781600 345319